D0745620

If I Were the

President

by Thomas Kingsley Troupe   illustrated by Heather Heyworth

Special thanks to our adviser for his expertise:

Terry Flaherty, Ph.D., Professor of English
Minnesota State University, Mankato

WITHDRAWN

Picture Window Books
Minneapolis, Minnesota

Editor: Shelly Lyons
Designer: Tracy Davies
Page Production: Melissa Kes
Art Director: Nathan Gassman
Editorial Director: Nick Healy
Creative Director: Joe Ewest
The illustrations in this book were created with traditional
drawing and digital painting.

Picture Window Books
151 Good Counsel Drive
P.O. Box 669
Mankato, MN 56002-0669
877-845-8392
www.picturewindowbooks.com

Copyright © 2010 by Picture Window Books
All rights reserved. No part of this book may be reproduced without
written permission from the publisher. The publisher takes no responsibility
for the use of any of the materials or methods described in this book, nor for
the products thereof.

Printed in the United States of America.

 All books published by Picture Window Books are manufactured
with paper containing at least 10 percent post-consumer waste.

Library of Congress Cataloging-in-Publication Data
Troupe, Thomas Kingsley.
If I were the president / by Thomas Kingsley Troupe ;
illustrated by Heather Heyworth.
p. cm.
Includes index.
ISBN 978-1-4048-5533-5 (library binding)
ISBN 978-1-4048-5712-4 (paperback)
1. Presidents—United States—Juvenile literature. I. Title.
JK517.T76 2009
352.230973—dc22   2009003298

If I were the president, I would have the most important job in the United States government!

If I were the president, I would live in the White House. It's the most famous house in the United States! My chefs would make me anything I wanted to eat.

If I were the president, I could play fetch with Patches on the lawn.

I could swat the ball around on my own tennis court.

Smack!

I could splash in the huge fountain just for fun.

Splash!

If I were the president, I would sit in the Oval Office at the desk where past presidents once sat. I would sign or veto bills.

 A bill is a new law under consideration. It passes through a branch of the government before it is presented to the president. The president then decides if the bill should be made into a law.

If I were the president, I would also be known as the Commander in Chief. I would decide if we needed our armed forces, such as the Army or Navy, to fight here or in other countries. I would do everything I could to keep our nation and the rest of the world safe.

George Washington and James Madison were the only two presidents in our nation's history to have acted as Commander in Chief on the battlefield in times of war.

If I were the president, Secret Service agents would follow me wherever I went. They would protect me from harm. I would ride in an armored car built just for me.

The president's limousine is often called Cadillac One. It has a protective body, underside, and windows. The tires are designed to continue to roll, even if they are flat!

If I were the president, I would travel in my own airplane. I would zoom to different countries to meet people from around the world. I would try to make sure we all got along.

Take off!

The president's airplane is called Air Force One. It is almost like a White House in the sky. It has offices in which the president and his staff can work. It also has an exercise room, bedroom, and bathroom built just for the president.

If I were the president, people would listen to me talk. I would speak to millions of people on TV, on the radio, and on the Internet. I would let everyone know how the country was doing.

If I were the president, I would host state dinners at the White House. World leaders, athletes, movie stars, and people from around the country would join me. We would talk, and eat the most delicious food!

20

If I were the president, I would do everything I could to protect our freedom. Millions of people would look up to me and trust me to lead them. I would love my very important job as the president of the United States!

How do you get to be the President?

It's not easy to become the president of the United States. For starters, you need to be at least 35 years old. You also must have been born in the United States and lived there for at least 14 years. Most people who want to become the president will work in a government office for a number of years before running for president. Past candidates were governors, U.S. senators, U.S. representatives, or other government and military leaders.

The president is elected by the people of the United States. An election is held every four years. People 18 years or older can vote. The election is held on the first Tuesday after the first Monday in November. During the year before the election, the presidential candidates travel across the country. They meet as many voters as they can and try to gain support. Once elected, the president begins his or her term on January 20 of the next year.

Glossary

Air Force One—any plane carrying the president of the United States

armed forces—a country's military forces, such as the army and navy

bill—a written plan for a law under consideration

Cadillac One—the name of the president's armored car

freedom—the right to do and say what you like

government—the group of people who make laws, rules, and decisions for a country or state

limousine—a long, fancy car

Oval Office—the official office of the president of the United States; it is located inside the White House

veto—the power of the president, governor, or an official group to keep something from being approved

To Learn More

More Books to Read

Buller, Jon. *Smart About the Presidents.* New York: Grosset & Dunlap, 2004.

St. George, Judith. *So You Want to Be President?* New York: Philomel, 2004.

Stier, Catherine. *If I Ran for President.* Morton Grove, Ill.: Albert Whitman, 2007.

Internet Sites

FactHound offers a safe, fun way to find Internet sites related to this book. All of the sites on FactHound have been researched by our staff.

Here's all you do:

Visit *www.facthound.com*

FactHound will fetch the best sites for you!

Index

Look for all of the books in the Dream Big! series:

If I Were a Ballerina
If I Were a Major League Baseball Player
If I Were an Astronaut
If I Were the President

31901046923357